To Matt – D.K.

Thanks to the Dyson Design
Department for designing the Edison toy.
Sorry it was the wrong way round. – M.P.R.

First published in Great Britain in 2003 by
Frances Lincoln Limited, 4 Torriano Mews,
Torriano Avenue, London NW5 2RZ

www.franceslincoln.com

British Library Cataloguing in Publication Data available on request

ISBN 0-7112-1864-1

Printed in Singapore

1 3 5 7 9 8 6 4 2

EDISON'S
Fantastic
PHONOGRAPH

DIANA KIMPTON ✽ M.P. ROBERTSON

FRANCES LINCOLN

More than a hundred years ago, there was no
television and no radio. There were no videos
and no CDs. If you wanted entertainment,
you had to make it yourself.

Then Thomas Edison did something that
amazed the whole world. It happened in 1877,
at his laboratory in New Jersey, America.

Thomas Edison looked up from his work and smiled
at his daughter, Dot.

"Look," said Dot. "I've brought you a special pie
for lunch – I helped make it."

"Lovely," said Edison. "And while I'm eating, I'll show
you something exciting."

Edison took a long strip of paper with tiny bumps on it
and slipped one end underneath a lever on the bench.

"Now listen carefully," he said and pulled the whole strip
under the lever as fast as he could.

"It made a humming noise," said Dot with surprise.

"It's because the bumps made the lever go up and down
very quickly," said Edison. "The movement made the sound.
Now come with me and I'll show you something even better."

He led Dot over to a strange piece of equipment with a funnel and a cut-out paper picture of a man holding a saw.

"Watch the little man carefully while I shout into the funnel. But first of all you have to tell me what to say."

"*Mary Had a Little Lamb*," said Dot straightaway.

Edison took a big breath, put his mouth close to the funnel and shouted,

> *"Mary had a little lamb*
> *Whose fleece was white as snow*
> *And everywhere that Mary went*
> *The lamb was sure to go."*

As he spoke, the paper man jiggled about.

Dot squealed with delight. "He looks as if he's sawing wood," she said.

"And it was my voice that made him move," said Edison. "Sound can make movement and movement can make sound. Soon I'm going to use those two facts to make the most exciting invention you have ever seen."

"Oh, tell me what it is," begged Dot.

But Edison shook his head. "It's going to be a surprise," he said.

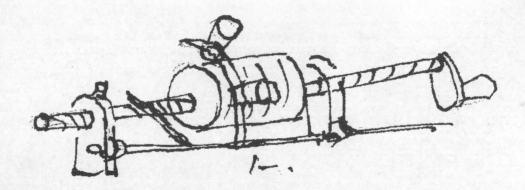

Edison worked hard on his new invention for weeks and weeks.
He drew diagrams in his notebooks and did experiments to test
his ideas. Sometimes he worked so hard that he stayed up all
night, then fell asleep in his laboratory.

The months went by and still the invention
wasn't ready.

"Have you finished the surprise yet?"
asked Dot as they walked together through
the autumn leaves.

"Not yet," said Edison.

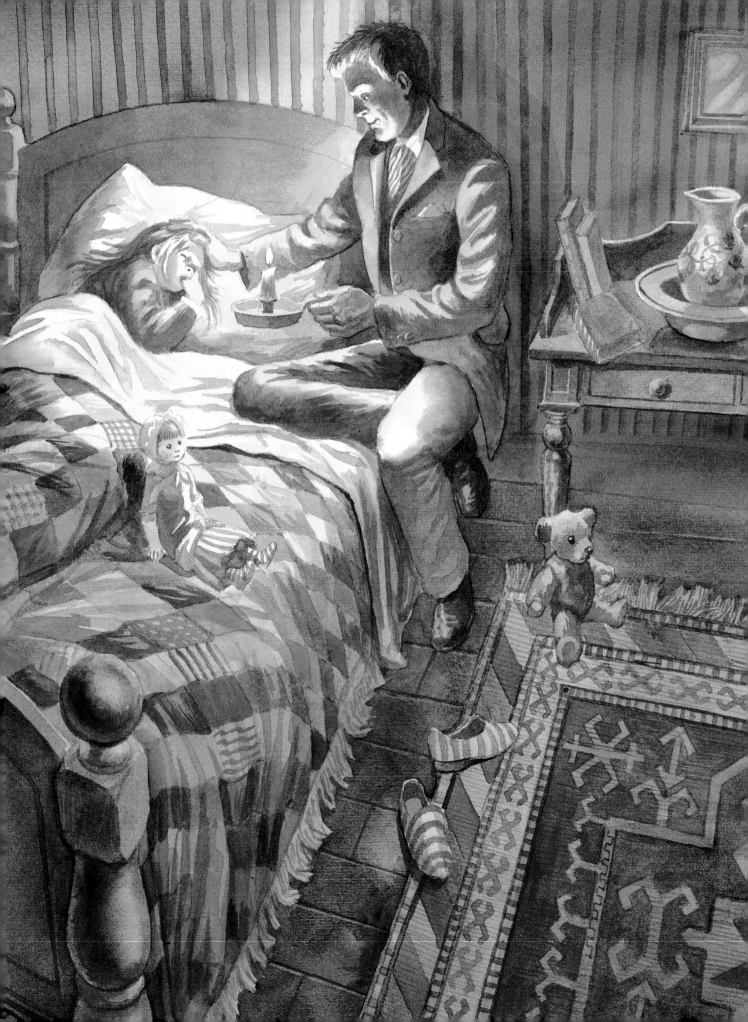

"Have you finished the surprise yet?" asked Dot as her father tucked her into bed a few weeks before Christmas.

"Very nearly," said Edison. He bent down to kiss her good night but she grabbed his hand to stop him leaving.

"Tell me a rhyme please," she begged.

So Edison began:

"Mary had a little lamb
Whose fleece was white as snow…"

Dot smiled, closed her eyes and was fast asleep by the time he had finished.

Edison was so keen to get back to work that he rushed downstairs, raced out into the cold, frosty air and ran the short distance to his laboratory.

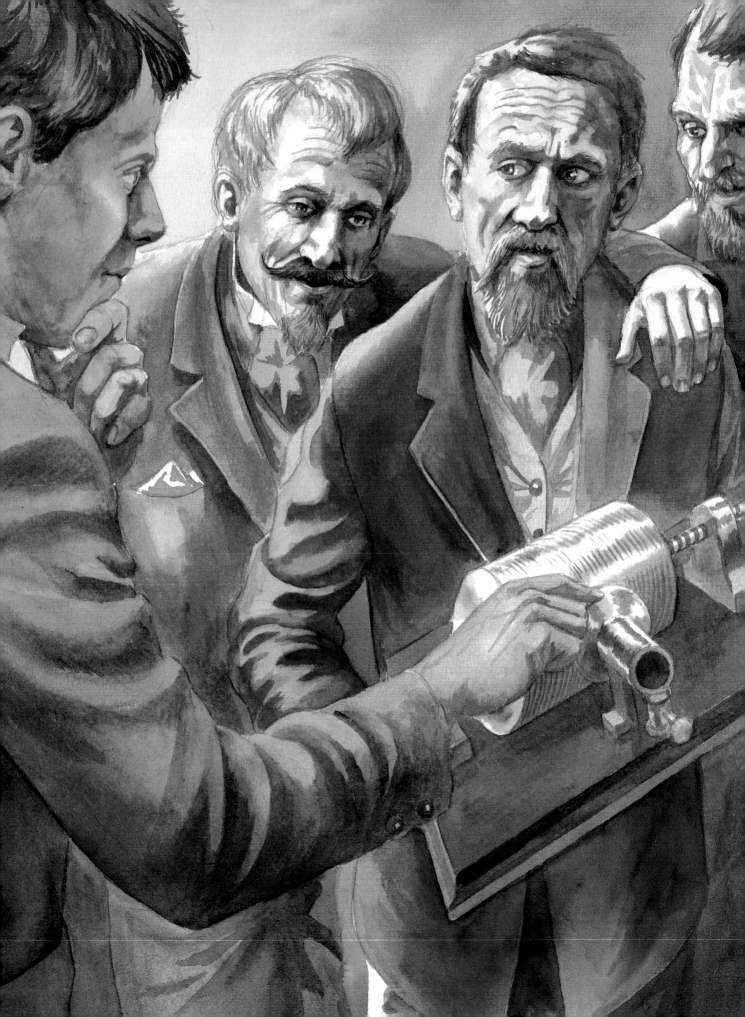

Everyone stopped what they were doing when he arrived.
A mechanic called John Kruesi held out a strange-looking object.

"I've finished your machine," he said. "It's exactly like your drawings."

"But what is it?" asked a man who had only just started work at the laboratory.

"I've called it a phonograph," said Edison. "If it works the way I've planned, it'll record my words when I speak and play them back exactly as I said them."

Everyone laughed.

"It'll never work," said John Kruesi.

Edison didn't mind them laughing. He knew he was trying to do something no one had ever done before, but he was sure it was possible.

He carefully wrapped a sheet of tin foil around the cylinder of the phonograph and adjusted a needle on the machine so it just touched the foil. Then he started to turn the handle, put his mouth close to the phonograph and shouted,

"Mary had a little lamb
Whose fleece was white as snow
And everywhere that Mary went
The lamb was sure to go."

Everyone laughed again at the sight of a grown man reciting a nursery rhyme. But they stopped laughing when he showed them the tiny scratches the needle had made on the tin foil.

"The sound of my voice made the needle move and the needle made a picture of the noise I made. Now let's see if we can turn that picture back into sound."

Nervously Edison made the final adjustments to the phonograph. The other men held their breath as he started to turn the handle.

As the cylinder went round and round, the scratches on the tin foil made another needle move.

To everyone's amazement, they heard *Mary Had a Little Lamb* again. But this time Edison wasn't saying anything – the words were coming from the phonograph. It had turned the movement of the needle into sound!

All the men went wild with excitement. They clapped and cheered and slapped each other on the back. The experiment was a huge success. Edison had recorded sound for the very first time.

For the rest of the night, they played with the new invention. They recorded people speaking. They recorded people singing. They even recorded someone playing the organ.

They didn't stop until morning came and they were all too tired to carry on any longer. But Edison still had one more thing he wanted to do before he went to bed.

He went home and fetched Dot.

"Go to the lab," he said, "and ask Mr Kruesi to show you the big surprise you've been waiting for."

He let her rush on ahead and go into the lab by herself. Then he peeped round the door and watched.

John Kruesi turned the handle of the phonograph and Dot's mouth dropped open with surprise as she heard her father's voice come out of the machine:

"Mary had a little lamb
Whose fleece was white as snow..."

"It's magic," cried Dot as she jumped up and down with excitement.

"No, it's not," said Edison, giving her a big hug. "It's science and it's going to change the world. There'll be talking books and talking toys, spoken messages instead of written ones and music to listen to whenever we like."

And Edison was absolutely right.

THOMAS ALVA EDISON was born in America in 1847. He didn't do well at school, so his mother taught him many of his lessons at home and it was there that he first discovered his love for science. Soon he was spending most of his spare time and pocket money carrying out his own experiments.

When he was 12, he started his first job, selling newspapers on a train. The work was easy enough to leave him with time on his hands, so he fitted out part of the baggage car as a travelling laboratory. Unfortunately, an accident with some of the chemicals started a fire and he lost his job.

Following this, Edison trained as a telegraph operator and many of his earlier inventions were designed to improve the way the telegraph worked. His daughter Marion and her younger brother Thomas were nicknamed Dot and Dash after the two morse code symbols.

Soon Edison was earning enough from his creations to live on, so he was able to concentrate completely on developing his own ideas and improving those of other people. He built a house and laboratory at Menlo Park in New Jersey and it was there that he developed his two most famous inventions – the phonograph and the electric light bulb. As a result, many people called him 'The Wizard of Menlo Park'.

Edison helped to change the world. Thanks to him and other scientists who built on his ideas, we can listen to music whenever we like and turn darkness to light at the flick of a switch.